IMAGES
of England

BUSHBURY AND FEATHERSTONE

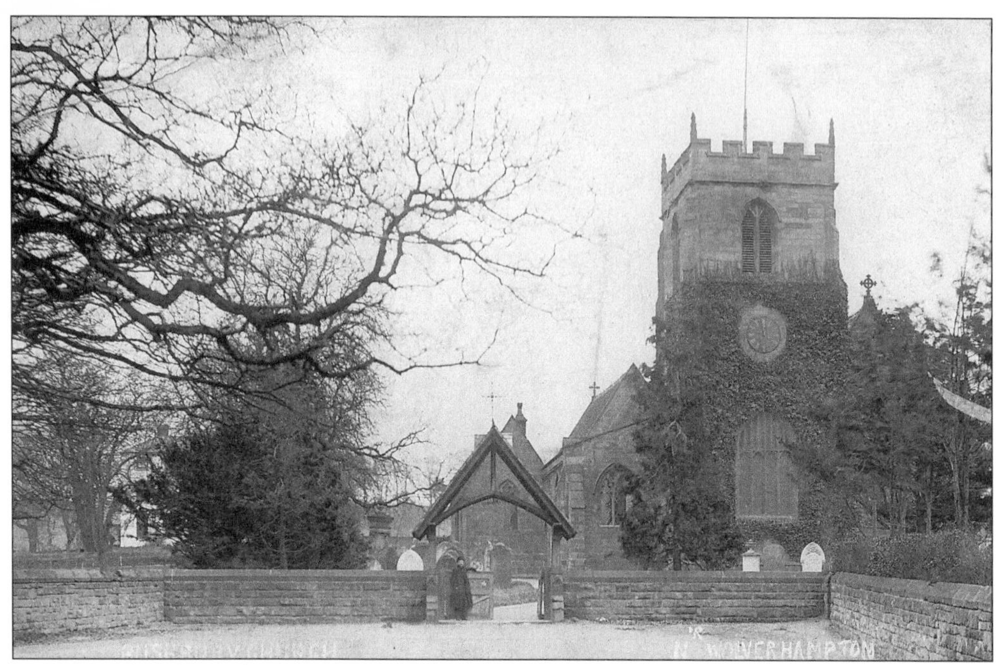

St Mary's church, Bushbury, at the turn of the century, with the lich-gate prominent. The ivy has now been removed from the stonework. Bushbury Hall can just be seen through the trees to the left.

Hilton Main Colliery and Brickworks in November 1957. Opened in 1924, the colliery led to the construction of Featherstone village for the housing of miners.

IMAGES
of England

BUSHBURY AND FEATHERSTONE

Compiled by
Alec Brew

First published 1999

Tempus Publishing Limited
The Mill, Brimscombe Port,
Stroud, Gloucestershire, GL5 2QG

ISBN 0 7524 1535 2

Typesetting and origination by
Tempus Publishing Limited
Printed in Great Britain by
Midway Clark Printing, Wiltshire

Bushbury and Featherstone is Alec Brew's seventh and final book in The *Archive Photographs* Series, chronicling Wolverhampton in a century of photographs.

Already published are:
Codsall and Claregate
Ettingshall and Monmore Green
Heath Town and Fallings Park
Penn and Blakenhall
Tettenhall and Pattingham
Willenhall to Horseley Fields

Also by Alec Brew in the same series:
Albrighton and Shifnal
Staffordshire and Black Country Airfields

In preparation:
Shropshire Airfields
Bridgnorth

Contents

Introduction 7

1. Bushbury 9
2. North Street 39
3. Waterloo Road 53
4. Dunstall 63
5. Fordhouses 71
6. Featherstone 79
7. Essington 105
8. Shareshill 121

Acknowledgements 128

The Wolverhampton lifeboat was given to the Royal National Lifeboat Institution. It was first launched at Bushbury Pool on 28 August 1866 but was lost at sea on 27 January 1883.

John Hayward and his family outside their shop, Essington Stores, in 1901.

Introduction

At the beginning of the twentieth century Bushbury was a tiny village but a parish with a huge area which encompassed Essington, Coven and many other scattered hamlets. Built below the brow of Bushbury Hill, St Mary's church was the centre of a very small collection of buildings that included Bushbury Hall and farm, and the village school.

A medieval route from Worcester to Stafford ran along the line of Bushbury Hill, but the later line of the Wolverhampton to Stafford road ran along the base of the ridge below Bushbury. This line was followed by the Staffordshire and Worcestershire Canal and later the railway. Therefore they all bypassed Bushbury which remained a quiet farming community.

It was the development of the railway industry in the nearby town of Wolverhampton, however, that was threatening the rural tranquillity of the parish. As the various railway companies built Oxley Sidings, the Stafford Road Works and Bushbury Shed, housing for the railway workers spread along Stafford Road, around Dunstall Hill, and brought further industry. Large industrial companies such as the Electric Construction Company, Guy Motors and Goodyear drew further workers to the area and the large planned housing estates of Low Hill were started in the 1920s, spreading the boundaries of Wolverhampton ever outward through Oxley and Fordhouses, and threatening Bushbury village itself. When housing construction continued after the Second World War Bushbury itself was finally engulfed, though thankfully the planners prevented building on top of the ridge, which remains a tree-lined landmark in the background of many photographs of the north side of Wolverhampton.

Further north than Bushbury lay the equally quiet village of Shareshill which served the estate of Hilton Hall, home of the Vernon family, and the local farms. On the other side of Hilton Park was the village of Essington, part of Bushbury parish until its own church of St John the Evangelist was opened in 1933. Essington was changed, not by the spread of its large neighbour to the south, but by the exploitation of the Hilton coal seam. Of the pits which were dug in the area, Holly Bank Colliery, which sprang from the liquidation of Essington Wood Colliery in 1895, came to dominate under the stewardship of John Charles Forrest, who became a great benefactor to the village.

When the Holly Bank Colliery Company decided to dig a new shaft to exploit the Hilton coal seam (the deepest on the Cannock Chase coalfield at 1,890ft) and Hilton Main Colliery was opened in 1924, it was J.C. Forrest, as a member of Cannock Rural District Council, who initiated the construction of 500 new houses at Featherstone to house the mine workers. The village of Featherstone, which was nothing more than a few cottages and farms with a population of 39 in 1921, became a community of nearly 1,100 people only 10 years later.

Since the closure of Hilton Main in 1969, Featherstone has probably grown even more quickly than in its first ten years, becoming a dormitory village for Wolverhampton though, like Essington, lying outside the town's boundaries and firmly in the county of Staffordshire. The village's name has become more widely known for the huge Royal Ordnance factory, built in the adjacent fields during the Second World War. Now much contracted and owned by British Aerospace, much of the depot has been given over to Featherstone Prison, which makes the village name even more nationally known.

Only the village of Shareshill, hidden just off the Wolverhampton to Cannock road, retains some of the former tranquillity which had once been enjoyed by Bushbury, Essington and Featherstone. Shareshill, though subject to a great deal of new house construction, still remains a village of one shop, a pub, a church and a village school.

The Electric Construction Company Inventor's Club with their latest brainchild, 'the first automatic nut cracker and space travel machine', in 1957. The ECC was one of the main companies in Bushbury for nearly 100 years.

One
Bushbury

Nowadays the term Bushbury is usually taken to mean the whole area of suburban Wolverhampton built on each side of Bushbury Hill, from Stafford Road on one side to Cannock Road on the other, with Bushbury Lane running between the two. In days gone by Bushbury was a large parish serving a rural community which contained several large manors including Bushbury itself, Moseley, Essington, Oxley, Elston, Showell and Wobaston.

In the 1920s the Low Hill Estate was laid out by the town planners of Wolverhampton and was heavily influenced by the garden village movement, which had had its beginnings in the town in Park Village. The streets were wide, the public areas spacious and new factories were largely kept separate from housing. Further estates were built after the Second World War, spreading suburbia further out and engulfing the last remnants of rural life.

The development stopped at Northicote Farm, which was bought by the Council and incorporated into a conservation area that included the top of Bushbury Hill itself and the fields that stretched to Moseley Old Hall.

A side view of Bushbury church. The present church was founded by Sir Hugh de Bushbury around 1350, but there had been a church on the site in Saxon times. Opposite the south porch is the base of a Preaching Cross, showing that worship took place on the site even before a church was built.

A view from the top of Bushbury Hill around the turn of the twentieth century. The church tower is in the trees to the left and Bushbury Hall is in the centre. The west side of the Hall dates from 1730, but the rest of the building is much older. King Charles I stayed there in May 1645 when a Civil War skirmish took place on Bushbury Hill.

Moseley Hall around the turn of the twentieth century. Largely rebuilt in the early eighteenth century, the Hall was the home of the Moseley family, later replaced as Lords of the Manor by the Horton family.

The terraced houses of Wolverhampton had spread to the lower part of Bushbury Lane when this photograph was taken just before the First World War, but had a long way to go to reach the village of Bushbury itself.

Moseley Court, which lay a quarter of a mile to the north-east of Northicote Farm, at the turn of the twentieth century. It was built between 1815 and 1821 by Sir Thomas Whitgreave, a member of the Catholic Whitgreave family who had owned Moseley Old Hall. Moseley Court was demolished in the 1960s after being vandalized.

Bushbury church at the turn of the twentieth century when it was still a rural church in a tiny village and still covered by ivy. The church had been extensively rebuilt during Victorian times, and the lich-gate had been presented by Miss Theodosia Hinckes in 1863.

This view of a footbridge over the stream to the north-east of Northicote Farm was taken around the turn of the twentieth century, though the crossing still exists today. The gentleman in the background can also be seen in the photograph of Moseley Hall on p. 10.

'Honest' Tom Parker is in the centre on one of the first electric vehicles, made by his Electric Construction Company at Showell Road, Bushbury, in 1898. Apprenticed in the Coalbrookdale Ironworks, he later moved to Wolverhampton and established a horseshoe makers in Commercial Road. He became a pioneer in the construction of electrical generating equipment and founded the ECC in 1880 with Bedford Elwell, a well-known inventor.

The lower part of Bushbury Lane before the First World War, when the local children were still able to play in the road, spinning the hoop.

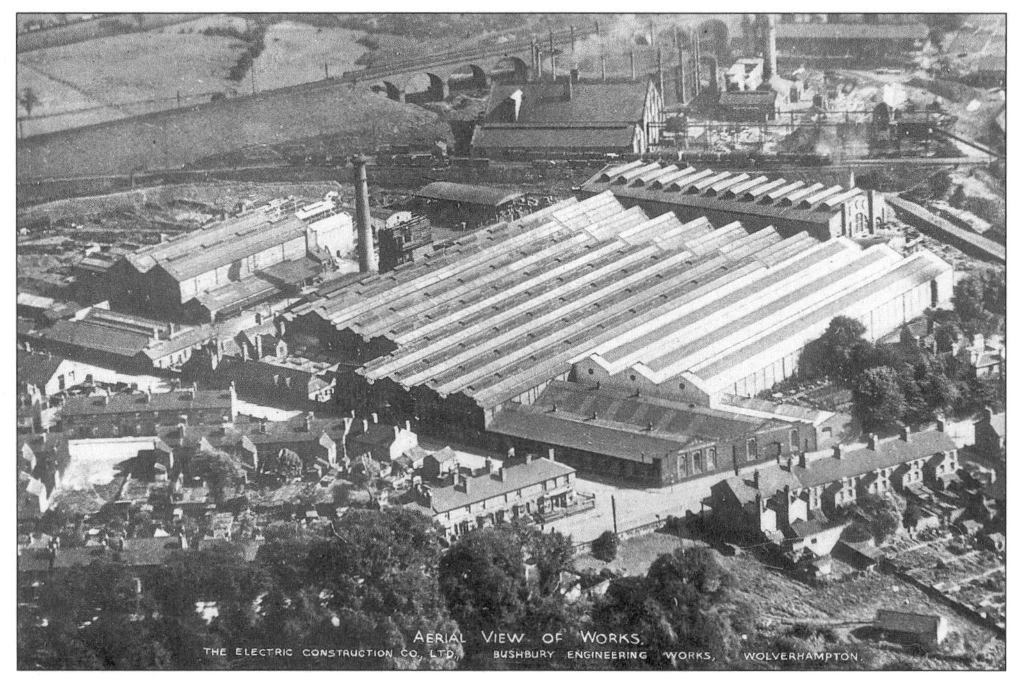

An aerial view of the Electric Construction Company which, by the start of the twentieth century, had become a major supplier of electrical equipment, both for generating electricity and for equipping many tramways and the pioneering submarine *Nautilus*.

A view inside the No. 5 erecting bay at the ECC, Bushbury, in 1902.

Workers from the New Erecting Shop at the ECC in 1908. Fifty years later it was still called the 'New Shop'.

Members of the committee of the Dumbell Comforts Fund at the Electric Construction Company during the First World War.

The ECC office football team from well before the First World War. Back row, left to right: E. Elton, R. Brown, A. Wilkes, R. McHugh, J.L. Roberts, C. Hawley, A. Preece. Front row: F. Rushton, D. Dunn, A.C. Grey, E. Humphries, C. Perks.

In 1913, just around the corner from ECC, Sidney Guy opened his truck factory in Park Lane, which became a big employer in the area for the next sixty years. This is the bus erecting shop in the 1920s.

Railway Terrace on Fordhouse Road, which runs parallel with the railway, off Bushbury Lane.

The Bushbury War Memorial gates presentation by T. Jones Esq. in 1921.

The Goodyear football team from the 1930s was good enough to offer professional players like Bill Paterson of Cowdenbeath a job in the factory just to get their footballing talents. Back row, left to right: W. Caddick (manager), S. Beddoe, F. Ward, T. Goodall, G. Botrill, E. Davies, G. Sproson, A. Bradley, F. Ibbs, J. Osborne (secretary), W. Chilton. Third row: A. Tomlins, W. Campbell, H. Lawley, G. Harris, H. Harrison, W. Powell, J. McLean (captain), S. Jarvis, D. Tranter, K. Walker (personnel manager), W. Gibson. Second row: F. Rans, A. Paterson, D. Livingstone, W. Owen. Front row: H. Grafton, J. Masters, S. Bailey.

The 21st Home Guard Company at Goodyear's factory in 1942.

The Electric Construction Company Home Guard in 1943. The sailor looks a little out of place. His name was McGowan and he happened to be home on leave, visiting his old mates in the factory as well as his brother, who is sitting next but one to him. Immediately behind the sailor is Ted Evans.

The Goodyear 'Tube Roomers' in 1943, when a great deal of female labour had been taken on during the war. Goodyear had started building their new factory on Stafford Road in 1927, and by July 1929 had built one million tyres.

The VE Day street party in Morrison Avenue, Bushbury.

The British contingent to the Goodyear 50th Anniversary celebrations in Akron, Ohio. There were twenty-one in all from Wolverhampton, but two are missing from this picture. Sixth from the right on the front row is Mr Lichfield, the president of Goodyear, and over his right shoulder is Jim Stanley. Fourth from the right is Walter Hazelit, the managing director in Wolverhampton.

The Coronation Day street party in Fifth Avenue, Low Hill.

Workers from the Park Lane bus depot having a Christmas dinner at the Spread Eagle, Gailey, in 1948.

This new housing was built just after the Second World War and expanded right through Bushbury. These houses are in Bentley Road.

The Bushbury Arms just after the war. It was built at Showell Circus in the 1920s to serve the new Low Hill Estate.

Much of the post-war housing built in Bushbury was prefabricated. These buildings are in Wentworth Road.

Workers and staff at the Electric Constuction Company in Bushbury Lane in 1945. Seated third left is Mrs Taylor, fourth left is Mr Taylor, sixth left is Mr Murray (foreman) and seventh left is Edgar Swain (chargehand). At the front, first left on the grass is Raymond Parsons.

The 1939 ECC Bowling Club were champions of the Wolverhampton Private Greens League and of the Wolverhampton Works League, Third Division.

Edward George Evans, aged two, in 1928 outside Rose Cottage which was then on Cannock Road, opposite the end of Blackhalve Lane. His little brother George Henry is just coming out of the door. They were both named George because their father, Edward Evans, had had a few in the Pear Tree before he went to register their birth and became confused.

The Pear Tree United football team for the 1952-53 season, along with the landlord and his wife, Mr and Mrs Adey.

The teaching staff at Bushbury County Junior School in 1951-52. Back row, fourth left is Margaret Buckland and fifth left is Rita Povey. Seated, left to right: Priscilla Cole, Mrs Lewis, Miss Williams (headmistress), Christine Jones, -?-.

The Hilton Main Colliery and Goodyear fire fighting teams training together at Goodyear's in November 1953. The Goodyear men are in uniform.

A 1920s aerial view of the ECC Works to the left, with Dunstall Park racecourse the triangle in the background and Bushbury Pool in the foreground. Stafford Road runs through the centre of the picture with Bushbury Lane below it.

A row of terraced houses which ran at the back of Bushbury Lane near the Shaw Road junction. These are typical of the houses at the lower end of Bushbury Lane.

Children at Bushbury Old Council School in 1939 or 1940. Front row, first left is Raymond Parsons who had the same place in the 1945 ECC staff picture shown on p. 23.

Bushbury Scout Troop marching away from the church in 1954.

A well-attended local wedding at Bushbury church in the 1950s.

The Butler's Arms was one of several very large pubs built to serve the new Bushbury estates. Opened in 1937, it is shown just after the war with Bushbury Lane running to its right. The Butler's Arms was knocked down in the early 1990s and replaced by a Kwik Save supermarket.

An unusual reunion inside the Butler's Arms in 1975. These are members of Popski's Private Army, a behind-the-lines unit like the SAS which was led by Lt-Col. Popski in North Africa and Italy during the Second World War. Seventeen former comrades attended including organizer Ben Owen on the extreme left, who was Wolverhampton born and bred. Holding the drawing is Ron Terill who was researching a script for a film on the PPA.

Engine 49446 outside Bushbury Shed in 1963. The railways dominated the Bushbury area with the shed part of the London and North Western Railway System. The LNWR line, which runs parallel with Bushbury Hill, was an awkward barrier as all the road bridges were single track, the line being built through a strictly rural area. They all remain, even the one on Elston Hall Lane, though a new dual carriageway bridge has been built alongside it.

The LNWR Double Home House on Bushbury Lane was built in 1905 to house train crews away from home, and had a resident cook/housekeeper. The Stafford Road Gasworks are visible in the background.

The Bushbury Engine Shed in 1963. The shed was built alongside Bushbury Lane in the 1850s, but a bingo hall and industrial units now occupy the site.

The 1955 football team from the Manley & Regulars brass foundry of Showell Road. Back row, left to right: Vic Lees, -?-, Brian Fincher, Tony Churm, Jimmy Cox, Jim Pemberton, Gordon Prosser, Sid Hewitt, -?-. Front row: -?-, -?-, Mick Holt, Henry Pool, Mr Hayes, Brian Clifton.

Contestants in the Electric Construction Company Personality Girl Contest in 1964. They are posing by the lily pond on the ECC sports ground. The contest was held at the ECC Dance in the Wulfrun Hall and was won by Mary Poole aged seventeen of the Typing Pool, who is third from the right on the front row.

Bushbury County Junior School football team in 1967, after beating Eastfield 1-0 in the final of the Blakemore Cup. Back row, left to right: Steven Holloway, Malcolm Murdin, Michael Vienas, Colin Johnson, Steven Davies, William Bailey. Front row: Brian Griffiths, Bryan Thursfield, Steve Felton, Billy Willington, Phillip Byrne.

Northicote School were Under 14 League Champions in 1982. Back row, left to right: Mr Brian Griffiths, David Crisp, Steve Arnold, Karl Edwards, Michael Brown, Neil Platt, Kevin Cummings. Front row: Robert Trickett, Lee Southwell, Frank McDermott, Paul Kennedy, Keith Williams, David Whitehouse, James Thomas. The link between these two pictures is Brian Griffiths who was a pupil in one and a PE teacher in the other.

Children and parents watch the Punch and Judy show at the ECC Sports Day in 1962.

Staff at Whitgreave Primary School in the early 1990s. Back row, left to right: Wendy Matthiason, Margaret Sexton, -?-, Barbara Parr, Jo Kibble, Liz Squire. Front row: Olwen Worrallo, Margaret Hinett, Tina Morris, Barbara Farrow, -?-, Nan Leach.

A 30ft model of HMS *Collingwood* was built by Collingwood Infant School in 1975 to celebrate the school's twenty-fifth anniversary: it opened as Bushbury County Primary School in 1950. The model is on a float passing through Heath Town during Wolverhampton's Fiesta Week and won second prize in the carnival.

Wolves' player Steve Kindon plants a shrub at Collingwood Infant School as part of the school's Silver Jubilee celebrations in 1977. The children gave a penny each towards the cost.

Children of Collingwood Infant School make the annual trek to the top of Bushbury Hill in the 1980s. Wonderful views across Wolverhampton and into Shropshire are afforded from the summit on a clear day.

The retirement presentation of Harry Jones in January 1982 by members of the Maintenance Department, after many years at the Electric Construction Company.

An aerial view of Collingwood Infant and Junior Schools, with Bushbury Lane running by the church to the right and the prefabs next to School Lane on the left. Northicote School is in the top left-hand corner.

One of the classes at Collingwood Infant School in 1996 gathered to look at the helicopter which took the previous picture. The class teacher is Wendy Matthiason.

The Wolves' mascot 'Wolfie', a character who made the national news after an altercation with the 'Three Little Pigs' at Bristol City's ground. Here he is taking part in the 'Brave Boys of Bushbury Park' opening ceremony in September 1996.

Two

North Street

In days gone by the main route to and through the Bushbury area from Wolverhampton town centre was along North Street. As the name suggests this was the main route out of the town to the north and along it were many of Wolverhampton's most important buildings. These include the Town Hall, the Market Hall, the Wholesale Market and Molineux House, later the Molineux Hotel, the grounds of which became Wolverhampton's first park and then the site of Wolverhampton Wanderers' stadium.

Beyond the markets, which nestled in the shadow of St Peter's church, the street passed through an area of terraced housing and then became North Road. At Five Ways it joined Stafford Street and Waterloo Road, both originally secondary routes to the north, and became Stafford Road running along the foot of Bushbury Hill. When the Wolverhampton ring road was built in the 1970s North Street was cut into two parts, linked only by a pedestrian underpass, and one of the main routes out of the town had become just a couple of cul-de-sacs.

Third left is Bill Price, the landlord of the Colonel Vernon Inn on North Street, about to set off for an outing with his family around 1900. The Colonel Vernon was on the eastern side, nearly opposite Vincent Street, but was demolished in 1966. Bill Price was an immensely strong man who once won a bet that he could knockout a shire-horse with one blow, in the yard of the Blue Bull Inn on Bilston Road.

The visit of the Chinese Ambassador to Wolverhampton. On the steps of the Town Hall in North Street in 1902 is the mayor Theodore Mander and third from the left, with the grey beard, is Alderman John Marston, the founder of John Marston Ltd and the Sunbeam Car Co.

Bill Price driving a coach load of his regular customers from the Colonel Vernon Inn on one of their many outings to the local countryside.

The grounds of the Molineux Hotel, after becoming Wolverhampton's first park in 1866. The hotel was built in the eighteenth century as the home of Benjamin Molineux, a wealthy local ironmonger.

A balloon ascent from Molineux gardens in 1888. Many sporting contests were held there, particularly cycle races, and the occasional football match. Just before the turn of the century Wolverhampton Wanderers moved from Dudley Road and built their new stadium on the site.

Wolverhampton outdoor market, taken from North Street around the turn of the century. The indoor market and St Peter's are in the background.

Wolverhampton Indoor Market Hall, taken from North Street, with Cheapside running up to St Peter's church. The Hall was erected in 1851 and demolished in the 1960s when the town's planners deemed a distant site by the Penn Road was a better place for the markets.

The opening of the west front improvements to St Peter's church in 1908.

The 'Civic Goodbye' to the 6th South Staffordshire war recruits on 5 October 1914. The mayor and aldermen are on the steps of St Peter's west front, with the Retail Market Hall behind the assembled troops and the Wholesale Market in the background. For many of the men in the picture it will have been a permanent goodbye.

The small group of buildings at the top of North Street included Kidson's general store for many years. Kidson's had another shop at the bottom of North Street. This photograph shows the staff of the top shop in 1955. The building was later occupied by TSB.

The Chequer Ball public house on North Street was conveniently sited to draw trade from the Wholesale Market next door and the retail markets over the road.

Many of the market stalls were family businesses of long standing. This picture shows the fish stall of George Summers & Sons inside the market hall in 1953. The firm was founded as a butcher's by William Henry Summers and was carried on by his son George (left) and his sons David (next to him) and George Geoffrey (who was serving in HM forces at the time). When George Geoffrey finally retired it brought an end to the firm after 108 years.

The outdoor market place was also a convenient place to hold a fair and this shows just such an event in 1908.

William Henry Summers with his little son George in the yard of his house, 34 St Peter's Square, in 1936. St Peter's Square was actually a short street, conveniently next to the market.

St Peter's Square in the early 1970s with the Wholesale Market to the right and St Peter's School to the left. Both have since been demolished and this street is now a pedestrian walkway.

The corner of North Street and Molineux Street in 1974, with the Molineux football ground just visible to the left.

Bill Price, son of the Colonel Vernon's landlord, marrying his wife Rose in 1922. The wedding party is in a coal yard in Vincent Street. Last on the right is Len Goodall, licensee of the Union Inn on Broad Street, which was known at this time as The Bridge. Many years later this coal yard was the site of the last working blacksmith in Wolverhampton.

A view across North Street in 1976 when all of the houses were empty and about to be knocked down to make way for an Asda supermarket.

A former lock works on the corner of Birch Street and North Street, just before its demolition in 1974, when it housed smaller companies including E. Mayes' electrical firm.

This terrace of three-storey houses was on the eastern side of North Road and is shown in 1974 just before demolition.

A 1974 view of Vincent Street, which was typical of the terraced streets that surrounded Molineux and many other football grounds around the country. This was demolished to make way for the John Ireland Stand and car park.

The Wholesale Market in 1974 when the retail markets had already been moved to their distant location by the ring road and their former site had become a car park.

St Peter's School, next to the College of Technology, in 1973 before it was demolished to make way for the expansion of what had become Wolverhampton University. By that time there were no children living anywhere near the school.

One of the major buildings on North Street is the Civic Hall, which was built between 1936 and 1938, serving many functions including the home of Boulton Paul Aircraft's annual dance, which is shown here in the 1960s.

The lower end of Molineux Street in 1976, now demolished and occupied by the Molineux club shop and car park.

Birchfield Street School in June 1976, which filled the gap between Birchfield Street and Red Cross Street.

A view of Wolverhampton's Town Hall which was only briefly available between the demolition of the Market Hall and the construction of the new Civic Centre on the same site from 1974.

Three
Waterloo Road

In days gone by Waterloo Road was one of the most elegant urban thoroughfares in Wolverhampton, but in recent years has been largely taken over by offices, converted either from Victorian houses or new blocks. Running from Darlington Street to Five Ways, where it joined North Road, it remains to this day one of the main routes from the town centre to the north via the Bushbury area.

It was chopped in two by the ring road but unlike North Street, which was permanently separated, it was merely interrupted by traffic lights. The main institution along its length remains Molineux football stadium, but two new ones have recently appeared at its northern end. Serving as major landmarks on the northern approach to the town are the Wolverhampton University halls of residence and the new mosque on the site of the former Christchurch.

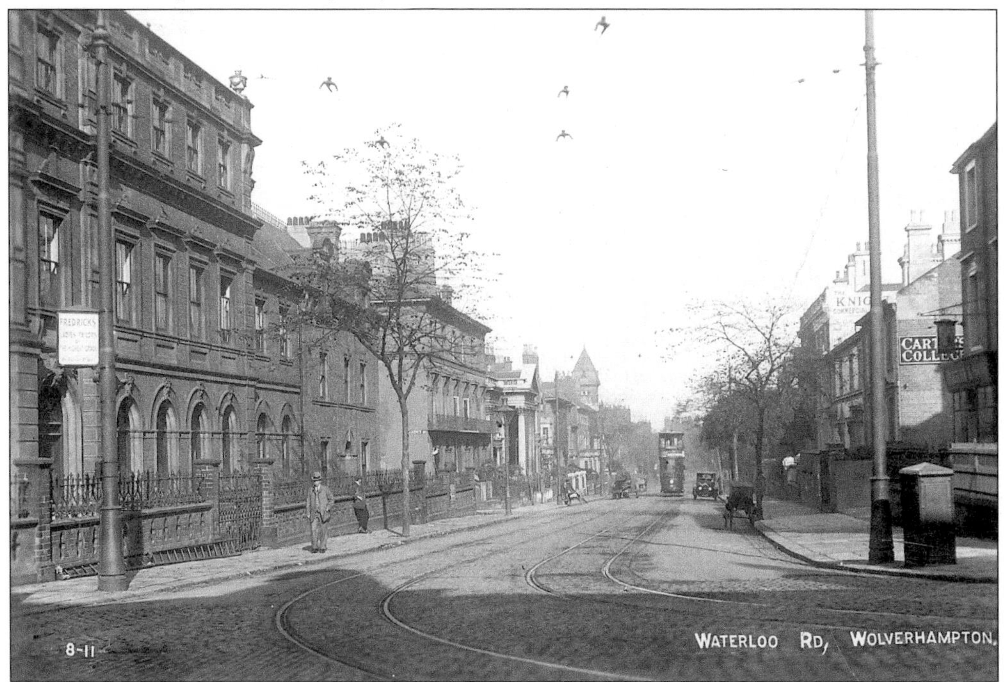

The start of Waterloo Road in the 1920s, where the tram tracks turned off Darlington Street. The building to the left is now more familiarly known as the site of the concrete Gas Board showrooms, though the Gas Board moved out many years ago.

A little further along Waterloo Road, the Baptist chapel is on the left, one of a small number of Victorian buildings in this part of the road which have now been demolished.

Wolverhampton Wanderers FC in 1899, ten years after moving their home to Molineux, with its entrance on Waterloo Road. They had by then adopted their famous colours of gold and black, but worn in stripes.

The lower part of Waterloo Road around the turn of the century when the Lorain system trams (surface contact) were still running. The tracks forked just before Molineux, one line going on to Bushbury and one swinging left down Newhampton Road, built first to take visitors to the 1902 Industrial Exhibition in West Park.

Looking down Bath Road, which ran from Waterloo Road to Chapel Ash, but has now largely been removed to make way for the ring road. The Catholic Apostolic church is on the right, with St Mark's in the distance.

A view of Bath Road, looking in the opposite direction to the previous picture, towards Waterloo Road. The Municipal Baths lay in Bath Avenue, just off Bath Road.

In 1902 Wolverhampton held a mammoth Industrial Exhibition at West Park. These impressive pavilions were erected in fields between the park and Newhampton Road, where visitors arrived on trams coming down from Waterloo Road. The nearest pavilion is the Canadian Pavilion and next to it is the Industrial Hall.

Within the park were a number of rides including a water chute into the lake. This spiral railway was a very early roller coaster.

There were a number of catering facilities for the tens of thousands of visitors including the Connaught Restaurant. Unfortunately the 1902 Industrial Exhibition was a financial failure and cost the town a great deal of money.

The elegant railings surrounding West Park were used as a backdrop for company photographs of many of the vehicles made in Wolverhampton before the Second World War. These, however, are a group of private motorcyclists about to set off on a trip to the depths of Shropshire on their A.J.S.'s and other motorcycles.

The Christmas party for the staff of the Wolverhampton Engraving Company of Gatis Street, held in the Victoria Hotel in 1928.

The hockey team of the Municipal Secondary School, Newhampton Road, for the 1933-34 season. They played on the fields opposite the school, where the pavilions of the 1902 Industrial Exhibition had been sited.

The small Baptist chapel that used to be nearly opposite the Molineux grounds on Waterloo Road. It has now been replaced by a new building and a new denomination.

Christchurch was at the very end of Waterloo Road, with Dunstall Road running to the right. A large mosque now stands on this site and the shops to the right have made way for a DIY superstore. This junction is known as Five Ways, even though six roads meet there.

The former Christchurch vicarage in 1974. By this time it had become a mosque, which has now been replaced by a purpose-built mosque next door.

The Red Roofs Hotel at the corner of Staveley Road and Waterloo Road. It is now known as The Goalpost.

Molineux football stadium in 1962, taken from one of the floodlight pylons on the occasion of a visit by Her Majesty the Queen, with the Waterloo Road Stand to the right and the South Bank to the left.

The old Waterloo Road Stand at Molineux, with the main entrance gates and the players' entrance further down. This has now been replaced by the impressive Billy Wright Stand.

Will we ever see this again? The Wolves playing Manchester City in the top flight of English football. The players on view in 1981 include Paul Bradshaw, Emlyn Hughes, Kevin Reeves, Mel Eves, George Berry and Wayne Clarke.

Four
Dunstall

Drawing its name from Dunstall Hall and the estate of Dunstall Park, this area of the town became dominated by the railways during the nineteenth century. Their tracks criss-crossed the valley on viaducts and bridges as Wolverhampton became one of the major railway centres of the country. Oxley Sidings and sheds on one side of Dunstall Park were faced by the GWR's Stafford Road Works on Dunstall Hill.

Dunstall Park itself became the town's racecourse in 1888, replacing one where West Park was built. It remained almost unchanged for over 100 years before massive redevelopment in the 1990s led to it becoming Europe's first floodlit racecourse. In 1910 the Racecourse Company allowed its use, horse-racing permitting, as one of the country's first airfields and it continued to be the town's airfield until after the First World War.

Eventually Dunstall Hall was demolished to make way for the new Courtaulds' factory alongside the racecourse but Oxley Manor, just the other side of the Birmingham Canal and linked by a bridge, had survived, though converted into flats and engulfed by houses.

No. 25 Ewins Street, Dunstall, on 18 January 1912. At this time it was the home of Granny Hardwick. Ewins Street was in an area of housing between Five Ways and Dunstall Hill where the Do It All store is now located.

Great Western Railway staff by the Lower Stafford Street signal box at Dunstall Hill. Standing first on the left is Mr Edward Hough. Dunstall was dominated by the GWR's Stafford Road Works.

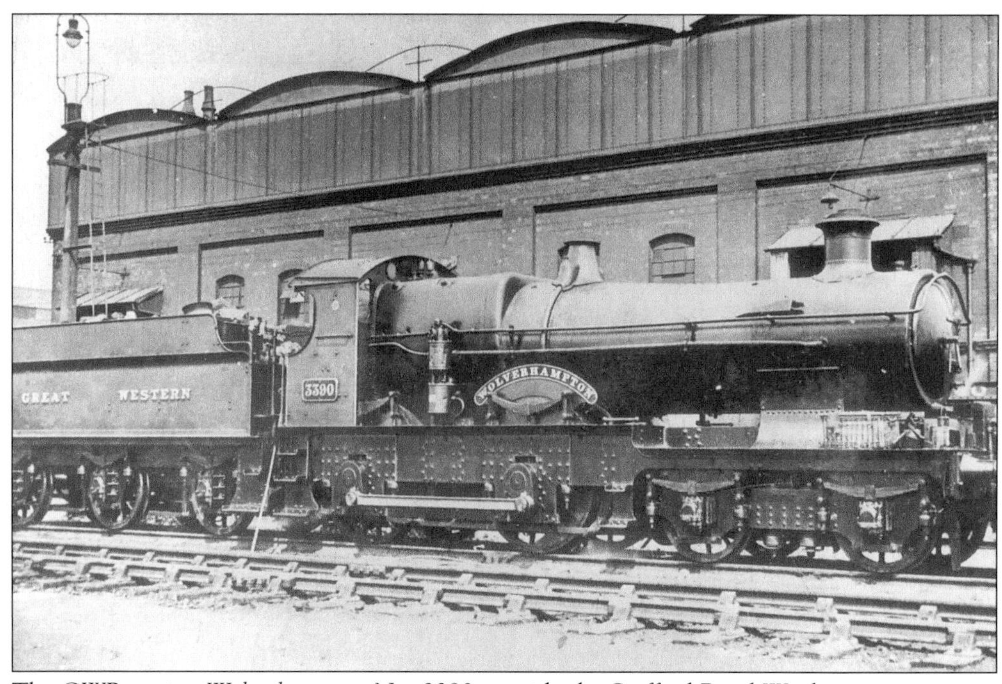

The GWR engine *Wolverhampton*, No. 3390, outside the Stafford Road Works.

A Short Bomber, serial 9357, on Dunstall Park racecourse in 1916. The Sunbeam Motor Car Co. built fifteen of these aircraft and Dunstall Park was used as the town's airfield at the time. Note the four bombs beneath the aircraft's wing and the mechanic working on the Sunbeam Ghurkha engine, a 240hp V12 side valve.

An Avro 504 on Dunstall Park in 1919. One of 541 Avros of this type built by Sunbeam, this was experimentally fitted with its own 100hp Dyak inline Six engine. Just such a Dyak-powered Avro 504 was the first aircraft used by Qantas in Australia.

The GWR Stafford Road Works' Home Guard unit. During the Second World War anti-aircraft units were stationed on the racecourse. These included rockets mounted on manually-operated turntables.

Children of the Baptist Tabernacle in Dunstall Road, *c.* 1945.

The Odeon cinema, next to Stafford Road at Dunstall, just after the Second World War when the film *Meet me at Dawn* was showing. This cinema was later renamed the Dunstall and became a bingo hall for a time before being demolished in the 1970s.

Stafford Road in 1970. This has recently been widened to a dual carriageway to complete the improvements from Five Ways to the M6 near Stafford.

The famous engine *King George V*, No. 6000, outside Stafford Road Works.

The office staff at Stafford Road Works around 1954, by which time they were all British Rail employees. Back row, left to right: Don Collingwood, Ray Ailes, Ernie Cheadle, -?-, George Smith, -?-, Reg Evans, John Smout. Front row: Monica ?, Elsie Gough, Mr Boulding, Beryl Cahill, Anita Casson.

A local train pulled by *Thornbridge Hall*, No. 6964, crossing Dunstall Viaduct en route from Shrewsbury to Wolverhampton Low Level on 20 September 1965.

A children's Christmas party at the Fitters Arms, Evans Street, in 1956.

A view over Stafford Road from Dunstall Hill in the 1970s. Gorse Brook Road is to the left and the buildings of the Electric Construction Company dominate the scene beyond.

Five
Fordhouses

Wolverhampton spread through the twentieth century from Dunstall along Stafford Road, through the suburbs of Oxley to Fordhouses. The housing in the area is typically 1930s semi-detached in style and industry is dominated by a few large companies. Goodyear's huge factory came to the town in 1927 on the site of a previous enamelware factory and further out Marstons moved to a new factory on Wobaston Road. Turner Engineering moved from the other side of town as well and H.M. Hobson's, now Lucas Aerospace, completed a little clutch of aerospace companies in the Fordhouses area.

This was appropriate as Wolverhampton chose Barnhurst Farm as the site for its new municipal airport, which officially opened in 1938. In 1936 Boulton Paul Aircraft moved from Norwich to a new factory alongside the airport, opposite Pendeford Mill, bringing with them 600 Norfolk workers, many of whom settled in the Fordhouses area. Though the new Pendeford housing estate has now been built over the airport, this little clutch of aerospace companies, with the exception of Turner's, still operates successfully.

Stafford Road as it was before the First World War, with the grounds of Oxley House to the right and the house which later became the Croft public house to the left. The tram is just by the end of Bushbury Lane and the ECC Goods entrance.

Lodge Road in Oxley is typical of the streets of 1930s-style semi-detached housing which spread through Oxley and the Fordhouses area either side of the Second World War. The Homestead public house is on the right.

Lord Gorell cutting the first sod in 1937 for an extension to the Boulton Paul Aircraft factory. The arrival of Boulton Paul from Norwich in 1936 had caused a big influx of Norfolk people into the Fordhouses area as well as providing employment for those already there. At the time the company was building Hawker Demons and was preparing for production of Blackburn Rocs and its own Defiant. On the extreme left is managing director Herbert Strictland, extreme right is Sir Charles Mander and alongside him is director, the Earl of Sandon. Fourth right, partially hidden is chief engineer J.D. North.

Barnhurst Farm at Pendeford with its moat and adjoining dovecote. Bought by the council, it served as a site for a major new sewage works and the town's airport. Only the dovecote now remains next to the pub which is named after it.

The final of the 100 yards flat handicap at the Boulton Paul Sports Day on 24 June 1944. During the war the workforce at Boulton Paul rose to nearly 5,000.

An aerial view of Pendeford Airport during the Second World War, with the Boulton Paul factory at the bottom and the RAF's airport buildings to the left. The grass airfield is camouflaged with painted 'hedgerows' and lies between Marsh Lane in the top left and the River Penk which runs parallel with the canal. Probert Road in Oxley is top right.

The visit of the King and Queen to the Boulton Paul factory in 1940. Managing Director Herbert Strictland is standing between them.

The Boulton Paul football team in 1945-46 when they were Wolverhampton Works League winners. Among the players are Len Roper, Dicky Holdsworth, Billy Hobbs, Tony Benjamin, Ginger Jones and Sid Will.

Sir Winston Churchill arriving at Pendeford Airport in 1949 for a mass election rally at Molineux stadium.

A Miles Gemini aircraft of Goodyear's at the Goodyear Air Races at Pendeford Airport on 12 June 1948. Several of the town's companies kept their own aircraft at the airport.

The newly widened Stafford Road at Fordhouses in 1961, with the Turner Engineering factory on the corner with Wobaston Road.

Celebrations in the Dowty Social Club, Fordhouses, in the 1970s. Standing are Len Roper (left) and Roy Pennick. Seated, left to right: Neville Webb, Maurice Mason, Ted Shaw, Les Jacques, Les Broadfield, John ?, -?-, -?-.

Oxley Moor Road when the old canal bridge was replaced in the 1970s.

Elston Hall Nursey, Fordhouses, in 1973 with Bee Lane field behind. On the steps is Diane Male and behind her Judith Howden.

Six
Featherstone

A pit village similar to many found in the North and the Welsh valleys, Featherstone was a tiny hamlet until Hilton Main Colliery was dug. Its larger neighbour Shareshill provided the local amenities of school, church, post office and shop; apart from the old Red, White and Blue pub alongside the Cannock to Wolverhampton road.

The colliery came and went, and Featherstone was forced to redefine itself, but the construction of the huge Royal Ordnance Depot alongside the village during the Second World War had already taken away reliance on coal mining and farming for local employment. With the rundown of the Royal Ordnance, part of its land was taken by the two new prisons, Featherstone and Brinsford, keeping the continuity of local employment.

Today the village is largely a dormitory for its neighbour, Wolverhampton, but safe from ever being swallowed up by the barrier formed by the new M54 motorway.

The makers of Featherstone. The directors of Holly Bank Colliery, Essington, decided to sink another pit at Hilton Main in 1924, thereby causing the construction of Featherstone village. Left to right: C. Ackroyd, Sir William Middlebrook, Norman Forrest (standing), Col. W.E. Harrison, J.C. Forrest.

Hilton Main Colliery during sinking in the early 1920s, when a boiler house chimney was in use, later replaced by all-electric power.

The official opening of Hilton Main on 30 September 1924 by Mrs Harrison, wife of the chairman of the Holly Bank Colliery Company.

An aerial view of Hilton Main around 1930. Note that the boiler chimney has now gone. In the background is the new housing of Featherstone village, which was being built by Cannock Council to house the miners. The Methodist church, which was built in 1929, can just be seen.

The West and Deep junction near the pit bottom of Hilton Main. The $2\frac{1}{4}$ ton mine cars were introduced in 1954.

Just to show that there was life in Featherstone before the mine, this is the old Red, White and Blue pub before the First World War. It lay on the corner where New Road was later built and was part of the ruins of a larger house.

Some of the first pupils at Featherstone County Junior School in 1930. The teacher on the left is Mr Amison and on the right Mr Cooper.

The Butterfly Queen at the Methodist church just before the Second World War. The Queen is Sheila Nicholls and to her left is Les Nicholls as a bridesmaid. On the right of the 'Ogre's Servant' in the mask is Maud Nicholls and on the extreme left is Maureen Nicholls as an elf.

A wartime production at Featherstone Community Centre with the figure of Britannia, played by Lily Bates, in the centre.

Early in the war the fields west of Featherstone were chosen for a new Royal Ordnance Depot. This aerial view from 300ft looks east at the construction on 15 April 1941. The railway runs across the bottom of the picture, with Cat and Kittens Lane above. In the top right-hand corner the circle of houses in North and South Crescent, Featherstone, can just be seen. This area of the depot is now occupied by Featherstone Prison.

The interior of the depot showing part of the internal railway system and the pipes of the steam main. There was also a hydrogen pipe running round the depot. The building in the background was 8F6, which was used for machining.

Next to Featherstone a camp called Brinsford Lodge was established for the workers in the Ordnance Depot. Those shown here are the cleaning and catering staff in the 1940s. The camp later became a teacher training college, particularly for Malaysian teachers, but has now been demolished.

Empty ammunition boxes stacked inside Featherstone Depot in the 1950s.

The Carnival Queen ceremony at the back of the Methodist church in 1933. Left to right: Irene Griffiths from Essington, Gwen Grice from Featherstone, Dorothy Cartwright from Cheslyn Hay, Peggy Byrd from Shareshill, Carnival Queen Verna Rowley, Eric Reynolds from Hilton, Alan Goodman from Featherstone.

Featherstone Methodist church women's outing to Southport in 1950. The church was the focus of all village activities until recent times.

The Methodist church just after the Second World War when the Victory Bell had been presented, dedicated on 2 May 1946 and inscribed, 'Victory 1945, Henry Whitehouse of Shareshill gave him'.

A Sunday school outing to Trentham Gardens in 1953.

A number of wooden huts at Westcroft were used as accommodation for Hilton Main miners for a long while, having been First World War ex-Army huts from Cannock Chase, and used initially by the men who sank the pit. The lady on the right is Mrs Davies holding her son.

National Coal Board Locomotive No. 2, built by Hunslet Engineering in 1952, crosses Blackhalve Lane.

Jack Mason, Frank Mason and Frank Cilfton collect their lamps to descend Hilton Main as employees of the Hilton Main and Holly Bank Colliery Company. They are starting the night shift on 31 December 1946.

Jack Mason, Frank Mason, Frank Clifton and a colleague finish their night shift on 1 January 1947 as employees of the National Coal Board: nationalization had come into effect at midnight.

A Featherstone County Primary School outing to Windsor Castle in 1956. The teacher is Mrs Cowan and among the pupils are Maureen Nicholls, June Whitehouse, Hazel Atkins, Pat Deakin, Pat King, Gwen Mansell, Isobel Hadley, Sylvia Hassell, Janet Carey and Kathleen Diggins.

A sewing class inside Featherstone School in the 1950s.

Hilton Main FC v The Red, White & Blue FC in the 1950s, played against a backdrop of the mine's spoil heap. Left to right: Terry Austin (on his backside), Derek Perks, Geoff Downes, Harold Austin (No. 10), Cyril Smith (goalkeeper), Harold Hurcombe, Joe Nicholls.

The Hilton Main Colliery Surface Ambulance team, winners of the J. Payton Cup in the 1950s.

The twenty-first anniversary celebration inside the church, with Jenny Lee MP cutting the cake. Jenny Lee was Member of Parliament for Cannock.

The Red, White & Blue, Featherstone, the 1-0 winners of the Wolverhampton Charity Cup in 1951, played at Molineux. Back row, left to right: Albert Baker, Reg Evans, Jimmy Whitehouse, Vic Parkes, Cyril Scott, Ernest Bate, Bert Davies. Front row: Ray Hurcombe, Ken Westwood, Joe Nicholls, Terry Austin, Sam Atkins and mascot Richard Williams.

Maypole dancing outside the church in the early 1950s. The trees of the Hilton Park estate are in the background, just beyond Cannock Road.

The harvest on Featherstone Hall Farm in the 1950s. Harry Rowbotham is driving the David Brown tractor and Ray Lunt is on the reaper and binder.

Westcroft United FC in the 1950-51 season. Based at the Pear Tree on Cannock Road, the team mostly consisted of miners and miners' sons. Back row, left to right: F. Richards, J. Hough, R. Peck, G. Ball, J. Regan, T. White, A. Goodman, Jo Johnson, M. Perks. Front row: J.R. Peck, S. Johnson, G. Appelby, F. Summerfield, A. Appelby, T. Peck, A.J. Peck and the mascot A. Harper.

Featherstone Blossom Queen on a parade through the village during the 1950s.

Building 8F6 at the Royal Ordnance factory in the 1950s. Part of the depot has now been taken over by Sandvik Ltd and the rest by British Aerospace, who have moved the entire operation into this building, which is now heavily rebuilt and renamed AP2.

The 'Gingham Girls' dancing troupe with their organizer Mrs Halfpenny in the Community Centre in the 1960s.

The Hilton Colliery Male Voice Choir in 1960. Back row, left to right: Len Herrington, Ivan Humphreyson, Edgar Fox, Sid Palmer, Joe Scarlett, Fred Bear, Arthur Hopcroft, Enos Bullen, Handle Palmer. Middle row: Len Mullard, John Griffiths, Charlie Nicholls, John Hawthorne, Bernard Hawthorne, George Evans, John Harley, George Perks, -?-, Reg Marsh. Front row: Eric Humphreyson, Joe Griffiths, Horace Evans, Frearic Cooks (mascot), Kitty Ridgway (pianist), Les Scarlett, Len Scarratt.

Hilton Main Colliery FC were winners of the NCB Cup in 1963.

The last shift at Hilton Main emerged from below ground on 31 January 1969. Left to right: Arthur Corbett, W. Mason, Phillip Harrison, Phillip Stewart.

Santa's Grotto at the church in the early 1970s. Left to right: Diane Dutton (Miss Featherstone), Santa Claus, Carol Wright, Louise Nicholls, Julie Davidson, Loraine Bush.

Mr Jones' class at Whitgreave Primary School in 1972. Featherstone County Junior School had now adopted the name of the Whitgreave family of Moseley Old Hall.

The 'Feathertones', the village's own pipe and drum band marching in the 1977 Silver Jubilee celebrations.

A street party in South Crescent, part of the village's 1977 Silver Jubilee celebrations.

Whitgreave School nativity production in Christmas 1981.

The sixtieth anniversary of the church. At the rear are Margery Evans and Verna Clewley (who was the Carnival Queen in 1933 when she was Verna Rowley, see p. 86), and at the front Vicki Amison cuts the cake. Seated on the right is the minister, the Revd Jeff Bramley.

Whitgreave School band. Standing, left to right: Lorraine Nicholls, Julie Cowell, Mark Bate, Margaret Felix, John Myrie, Sallanne Cowell, Jackie Turner, Miss Brigstock. Seated: Debbie Roberts, Celia Mills, Paula Workman, Karen Webb. At the front: Maxine Batchelor, Joanne Nicholls.

The anniversary of the church in 1990 with Louise Bradshaw on the piano.

A touch of the old days returns to the fields around Featherstone, with a steam traction engine rally on a local farm in 1993.

The nursery class at Whitgreave School in 1993.

The slow and steady approach to egg and spoon racing at Whitgreave School Sports Day. Natalie Brew is relying heavily on all her opponents dropping their eggs.

Sue Watts, the Health Visitor in Featherstone for many years, opens the Mothers and Toddlers Group at the church in November 1996. She is holding Courtney Hurcombe, the youngest baby. Standing behind her is Wendy Nicholls whose mother had been looked after by Sue Watts as a baby.

Preparing for the 1996 anniversary of the church opening.

A Whitgreave School Sports day and Danielle Brew shows fine style but not much speed.

Seven
Essington

Though Essington was a village with coal mines, unlike its neighbour Featherstone it was never solely a pit village. Though without a church – as it was part of the parish of Bushbury – Essington had long served the local agricultural community as a typical rural village with a school and shops.

The coming of the mines, for there were several in and around Essington, did have a large effect on the village, bringing miners and the railway to transport the coal. The rural traditions, however, continued as they do to this day, long after the mines have closed.

Like Featherstone, Essington has now become largely a dormitory village, but one with deeper strands of history to bind it together.

The old post office in Essington at the turn of the century when the village was still part of the parish of Bushbury.

A thatched cottage in Long Lane, Essington, at the turn of the century with a thatch in some need of repair.

A typical country scene in a lane near the brickyard in Essington showing the rural nature of the area despite the coal mines.

The Essington village band in 1900, showing the traditional connection between brass bands and pit villages was not confined to the north of England. The formation of the band was encouraged by J.C. Forrest of the Holly Bank Colliery, who revitalized the mine as well as village life.

Essington Mill at the turn of the twentieth century. It was built by 1681, but had ceased to work around ten years before this picture was taken. The stump of the mill still survives on Windmill Farm in sight of Bognop Road. It is the only surviving post-mill in Staffordshire.

Essington Vicarage, on Bognop Road, at the turn of the century.

The Old Farm, Essington, *c*. 1900. This was also known as Pool Farm and could be found on Bognop Road.

Colliers Castle, or 'Mockbeggar Hall', was built sometime between 1730 and 1780 and demolished around 1935. It is believed to have been lodging for retired employees of the Vernons of Hilton Hall, each of which had a large garden strip around the building, and it was later used by colliers.

George and Selina Nicholls outside their shop at 24 House Row in Essington, sometime before the First World War.

The Old Mitre Inn with, presumably, some customers standing outside around 1902. The terrace that lay behind it was known as Thirty House Row.

A cottage lying deep within Essington Wood at the turn of the twentieth century.

Class II at the National School, *c.* 1915. The school had been built in 1845 to cater for all village children up to the age of ten. Immediately behind the slate the boy is holding is Dyllis Holmes.

A popular lesson for the boys of the Church of England Mixed School in the 1930s was gardening and, besides its popularity, it was useful knowledge for a country lad to acquire.

Workers at Holly Bank Colliery, Essington, *c.* 1910. Until the opening of Hilton Main, Holly Bank was the premier pit on the Hilton coal seam.

The Sneyd Colliery, *c.* 1920. This began as the Essington Farm Colliery in 1873 but was sold to the Holly Bank Colliery Company in 1904 and renamed the Sneyd.

Ladies at a garden fête at Holly Bank House, the home of J.C. Forrest, around 1910.

A switchback railway ride at the Holly Bank garden fête of 1910. The ride was made from colliery cars running on timbers.

The distinctive signal box on Burnips Road and the Holly Bank locomotive No. 3 pulling some trucks in 1924.

Holly Bank Colliery during the miners' strike in 1926. Left to right: Ted Mills, Harold Taylor, Fred Beer, Harold Guest, Fred Paddock.

Outside Holly Bank House is Mr Maxwell the chauffeur in J.C. Forrest's Austin 12 Heavy, which had been built in 1922.

Bradley Hall Colliery, High Hill, Essington, in the 1920s. The colliery was known as 'The Nickett'.

Essington's cricket team from the 1920s. Back row, left to right: Walter Lathe, -?-, Cliff Roberts, -?-, William Sheratt, Alf Knight, -?-, -?-, Mr Onions the umpire. Front row: Joe Tucker, -?-, -?-, -?-, Mr Trow. On the ground is the scorer.

The Essington Prims football team of 1922-23 were the winners of the Wolverhampton Church and Chapel League Junior Division, the Sir Robert Bird Challenge Cup and the Beddows Memorial Cup.

Eli Ervans' shop in Hobnock Road, which was otherwise known as School Lane. Eli's did an excellent trade as the school tuck shop.

The wedding of Alec Mills and Daisy Tomkinson in Essington in May 1929. The wedding was at Bushbury church, but this photograph was taken at the rear of the Why Not Inn, Essington. Back row, left to right: Jim Hilditch, Alf Newall, Elizabeth Tomkinson, Sarah Tomkinson, Fred Tomkinson, Dolly Bird, Edward Mills, Elizabeth Mills. Centre: the newly weds. Front row: Ted Tomkinson, Madge Tomkinson, Lucy Tomkinson, Billy Bird, Maisie Tomkinson, Julia Mills.

No. 3 Platoon, the Essington Home Guard, photographed in front of Holly Bank Colliery. Back row, left to right: Ray Onions, Dennis Maiden, Joe Parkes, Ron Howarth, Bill Walkerdine, Willi Albert Danials, Idris (Slogger) Edmunds, Jack Hinks. Middle row: -?-, Ralph Hawkins, Harold Foster, Ben Tarbuck, -?-, Joe France, Arthur Corbett, Harold Lockley, Ernie Burns, Charlie Arrowsmith. Front row: Tom Nicholls, Jim Betterridge, -?-, -?-, Stan Brooks, -?-, Frank Gardner, Frank Hinks.

The Essington scouts at camp, c. 1920.

Essington Church of England Mixed School in 1949. Back row, left to right: Steve Harrison, Jack Wakelin, Andrew Morris, Horace Knight, Dennis Hughes, Bert Jeyes, Colin Barber, Bryn Whitehouse. Second row: Betty Aston, Pat Paddock, Betty Mason, Marj Dixon, Winnie Ridgway, Chris Asbury, Eileen Edmunds, Betty Upton, Tom Sylvester the headmaster. Third row: Trevor Blount, Carrie Arrowsmith, Iris Ward, Irene Powell, Margaret Clifton, Mary Burgess, Rita Powell, Brenda James, Roy Steadman. Front row: Ken Pace, George Marshall, Roy Worthington.

Yew Tree Drift Mine, Essington, in 1947 was one of the first projects of the NCB on its creation. Yew Tree was created by digging a cutting over the seam, constructing a concrete tunnel and then backfilling. The seams were no more than 300ft down, but Yew Tree was not a success because of excess water and was closed in 1950.

An aerial view of the Old Mitre Inn, to the right, and the Thirty House Row in the 1940s.

Essington Youth Club football team for the 1949-50 season.

Eight
Shareshill

The village of Shareshill has always served the local farming community and in particular the large estate of Hilton Park, home of the Vernon family. Of all the local villages Shareshill has changed the least over the century. The number of pubs has dropped from two to one, the number of houses has increased, but not by so many as its neighbours Featherstone and Essington, the school has expanded slightly and more than one local farm has succumbed to the plague of barn conversions, but otherwise village life remains as it was.

Bill Price, the landlord of the Colonel Vernon Inn, North Street, Wolverhampton, on an outing in the lanes near Shareshill at the turn of the twentieth century. His pub had been named after the Vernon family of Hilton Hall, Shareshill, and he kept a nearby farm at Coven.

A class at Shareshill School, *c.* 1910. This small village school has now been greatly expanded by the addition of a new wing.

A fancy dress contest inside Shareshill School in the 1920s. The contestants are all local villagers rather than pupils or teachers.

A reunion of former pupils outside the front door of Shareshill School around 1930. This corner of the school remains much the same today but the main entrance is now in a new extension.

Country dancing in a field by Shareshill church in the 1920s, with the participants wearing fancy dress.

The interior of St Mary's and St John's church as it appeared before the First World War.

Local people enjoy a Christmas meal at the village hall at Gailey. Most of these are believed to be workers from the Hamilton Park estate.

Hilton Hall, the home of the Vernon family for twelve generations from 1547, as it appeared in the 1920s. From 1958 it was owned by an order of nuns who kept it as a guest house for elderly people. It was put on the market in 1981 and bought by the Tarmac Group of Wolverhampton, who refurbished it as its head office, though putting it back on the market in 1999.

Employees at Hilton Hall about to embark on a charabanc outing in the 1920s from the rear entrance. The Hall and Hilton Park provided employment for a large number of local people from Shareshill and the scattered cottages of Hilton itself.

Uvedale Jones, head gardener at Hilton Hall, with his wife Harriett and their seven sons in 1908. Six of the sons were named Sidney, Clifford, Uvedale (junior), Walter, Albert and Tom. The name of the seventh, who was killed in the First World War, is unknown.

The bridge over the frozen lake in the grounds of the Hall, just before the First World War.

The North Lodge to Hilton Hall in the 1920s. It has recently been knocked down and replaced by a new house.

Two Hilton men, outside a cottage on the Hilton estate. Claude Andrew is on the left-hand motorbike.

The Elms public house, Shareshill, just after it was converted from a private nineteenth-century house by Butlers Brewery and opened on 29 September 1957. It replaced the Swan Inn, which was about 100 yards away. The first landlord was Mr Evans and his wife.

Acknowledgements

I must have talked to hundreds of local people while compiling the seven books in this series on Wolverhampton. Once more I have found people unfailingly helpful and willing to lend me their precious photographs – 230 in this book, around 1,500 in all – recording what it was like to live in Wolverhampton and its environs during the whole of the twentieth century.

In particular I have to thank Jim Evans for contributing the whole of the collection of photographs for the Essington section of this book as well as many in the Featherstone section. I found it impossible to consider trying to improve on his efforts over the years, and thank him for even letting me use a few which had already appeared in one or other of his two books with Michael Albut, *Essington* and *The People of Essington*; essential reading for anyone in the area.

I also have to thank, in particular, Trevor and Wendy Nicholls, not only for lending me many of their own pictures of the Featherstone area, but also for tracking down others for me. Harry Blewitt's marvellous collection of local postcards once more yielded quite a number and it's hard for me to have imagined completing these seven books without being able to draw on Harry's collection. In the same way it's hard to see how I could have done without David Clare's massive collection of photographs of the inner part of Wolverhampton as it appeared in the early 1970s. Ken Hale once again lent me some of his marvellous railway pictures.

Others I have to thank for lending me photographs and helping me in other ways, either directly or via others, (and I sincerely hope I have not missed anyone out) are: Mrs J. Allman, Tony Ball, Mr A. Bates, Mrs E. Benton, Miss E. Bickford, Jim Boulton, Peter and Maggie Brew, Margaret Buckland, Mrs Chittleborough, Bert Davies, Ted Evans, Brian Fincher, Linda Gayle, Brian Griffiths, Joan Hannan, Harry Jones, Norman Jones, Percy Kyte, John McNish, Jim Male, Gilbert Moody, Ben Owen, Raymond Parsons, Mrs W. Paterson, Alfred Peck, Gwen Porter, Fred Richards, Ian Robb, Brian Rollins, Jim Stanley, Kevin Summers, Stanley Webb, Val Willis of Collingwood Infant School and last, but never least, the indefatigable Wendy Matthiason.